# Jasper the Badger

Jasper the badger has a plan to get some peace and quiet so he can eat his piece of fu
his plan work?

This picture book targets the /j/ sound and is part of *Speech Bubbles 2*, a series of picture books that target specific speech sounds within the story.

The series can be used for children receiving speech therapy, for children who have a speech sound delay/disorder, or simply as an activity for children's speech sound development and/or phonological awareness. They are ideal for use by parents, teachers or caregivers.

Bright pictures and a fun story create an engaging activity perfect for sound awareness.

Picture books are sold individually, or in a pack. There are currently two packs available – *Speech Bubbles 1* and *Speech Bubbles 2.* Please see further titles in the series for stories targeting other speech sounds.

**Melissa Palmer** is a Speech Language Therapist. She worked for the Ministry of Education, Special Education in New Zealand from 2008 to 2013, with children aged primarily between 2 and 8 years of age. She also completed a diploma in children's writing in 2009, studying under author Janice Marriott, through the New Zealand Business Institute. Melissa has a passion for articulation and phonology, as well as writing and art, and has combined these two loves to create *Speech Bubbles*.

# What's in the pack?

User Guide

Vinnie the Dove

Rick's Carrot

Harry the Hopper

Have You Ever Met a Yeti?

Zack the Buzzy Bee

Asher the Thresher Shark

Catch That Chicken!

Will the Wolf

Magic Licking Lollipops

Jasper the Badger

Platypus and Fly

The Dragon Drawing War

# Jasper the Badger

## Targeting the /j/ Sound

### Melissa Palmer

Routledge
Taylor & Francis Group

LONDON AND NEW YORK

First published 2021
by Routledge
2 Park Square, Milton Park, Abingdon, Oxon OX14 4RN

and by Routledge
52 Vanderbilt Avenue, New York, NY 10017

*Routledge is an imprint of the Taylor & Francis Group, an informa business*

*British Library Cataloguing-in-Publication Data*
A catalogue record for this book is available from the British Library

*Library of Congress Cataloging-in-Publication Data*
A catalog record has been requested for this book

ISBN: 978-1-138-59784-6 (set)
ISBN: 978-0-367-64886-2 (pbk)
ISBN: 978-1-003-12677-5 (ebk)

Typeset in Calibri
by Newgen Publishing UK

# Jasper the Badger

**J**asper the Ba**dg**er loved to **j**ust sit and do nothing but eat. He enjoyed lots of different types of food, but especially porri**dg**e with **j**am and orange **j**elly.

Jasper would do**dg**e his friends, Imo**g**en the pi**g**eon and **J**enny the **g**iraffe, when he wanted to eat, as they were always so **j**umpy and fi**dg**ety and too excited.

One day **J**asper sat enjoying some **j**uicy fu**dg**e when along came **J**enny the **g**iraffe.

"I found you, **J**asper!" she squealed as she **j**umped with **j**oy.

**J**asper tried to think of a way to do**dg**e **J**enny, when he suddenly hit the **j**ackpot – he could hide and eat in peace and turn it into a game for **J**enny!

"You can't find me now!" **J**asper yelled and scurried away with his fu**dg**e.

Jasper jumped behind a garage. Just as he lifted his juicy fudge to his mouth, Jenny burst around the corner like a sledge hammer.

"I found you, Jasper!" Jenny jumped with joy.

"Try to find me again!" Jasper yelled, juggling his fudge as he ran away.

**J**asper **j**iggled his way under a old **j**umper. **J**ust as he started to nibble his fu**dg**e, **J**enny removed the **j**umper with a nu**dg**e.

"I found you, **J**asper!" **J**enny sang once again.

"Can't find me now!" **J**asper **j**umped away, clutching his fu**dg**e.

Jasper climbed up a huge orange tree. Surely Jenny couldn't find him there! Just as he imagined chewing his delicious fudge, Jenny's giant face appeared through the leaves.

"**J**enny! You are **j**ust too good at hide and seek. Let's **j**ust stop playing. Don't follow me again!" **J**asper stomped off in a ra**g**e.

Just as he was about to eat the rest of his fu**dg**e, he heard Imo**g**en the pi**g**eon chattering to herself. **J**asper quickly **j**umped over a he**dg**e to get away!

Oh no! **J**asper realised too late there was a hu**ge** hole just behind the he**dg**e …

… and he **j**umped straight into it, losing his fu**dg**e!

"Help! Help!" **J**asper cried, trying to **j**ump back out, but he couldn't – the hole was too big.

"**J**asper?" Imo**g**en called, nu**dg**ing her way through the he**dg**e.

"I fell into the hole and can't get out! Can you help me, Imo**g**en?" **J**asper asked.

Imo**g**en flew off to find **J**enny.

Just then, **J**enny's face appeared at the top of the hole.

"Please help me, **J**enny!" **J**asper cried.

So **J**enny leaned down with her hu**g**e head and long neck and grabbed **J**asper by the tail. With a quick flick, she managed to get **J**asper out.

"Thank you for rescuing me. I'm sorry I was mean to you, **J**enny," **J**asper said. "I **j**ust wanted to eat my fu**dg**e."

Imo**g**en landed beside **J**asper with something in her beak. It was **J**asper's lost fu**dg**e!

"Well, why don't you eat first, and then we can all play together?" said Imo**g**en. **J**enny nodded in agreement.

So **J**asper managed to eat his fu**dg**e in peace and quiet, and then he got to play with his friends.